IMAGES OF LABOR

IMAGES OF LABOR

Preface by Joan Mondale
Introduction by Irving Howe

Executive Editor   Moe Foner

Associate Editor
and Designer   Pamela Vassil

A Bread and Roses Book
The Pilgrim Press   New York

This book was produced as part of the cultural project of District
1199, National Union of Hospital and Health Care Employees,
RWDSU/AFL-CIO/CLC.

Supported by grants from National Endowment for the Arts,
National Endowment for the Humanities, Ford Foundation, J.M.
Kaplan Fund, Rockefeller Foundation, Samuel Rubin Foundation
and United Church Board for Homeland Ministries.

The publisher wishes to express appreciation for permission to reprint
copyrighted material.

Cover Art: Philip Hays

Library of Congress Cataloging in Publication Data

Main entry under title:

Images of labor.

   (A Bread and roses book)
   1. Labor and laboring classes—United States—Quotations,
maxims, etc.   I. Foner, Moe, 1915-
II. Vassil, Pamela.   III. Series: Bread and roses book.
HD8066.I37   305.5´6   80-28820
ISBN 0-8298-0433-1
ISBN 0-8298-0452-8 (pbk.)

The Pilgrim Press, 132 West 31 Street, New York, New York 10001

Dedicated
to the memory of
Joseph Cadden
and Stanley Glaubach;
and to the
thirty-two artists
who created
these images of labor.

CONTENTS

PREFACE

In 1979, the Bread and Roses project of District 1199, National Union of Hospital and Health Care employees, organized the historic exhibition, The Working American, which brought together paintings of Americans at work. As the show revealed, the image of the working American through art has varied as much as the role of the worker in society has changed. An eighteenth century portrait by John Singleton Copley of Paul Revere in his shirt-sleeves with the tools of his silversmith's trade conveys the dignity of the artisan-worker and the respect for an honest day's work that is so ingrained in our national consciousness.

Yet, in a twentieth century painting by Philip Evergood, called *Through the Mill*, the drudgery and dehumanization of a factory worker's life is starkly captured.

In *Images of Labor*, the latest project of District 1199's Bread and Roses culture program, the words of farm workers, union organizers, presidents and poets that capture the joys and sorrows, trials and rewards of working Americans are quoted alongside images by contemporary artists. Through the two-fold language of words and pictures, the portrait of labor is enriched and strengthened in a wonderful way. Thanks to the dedication and vision of District 1199 and The Pilgrim Press, the picture of the American worker that has been painted through the years is given new dimension and our nation's self-image is enhanced as well.

—Joan Mondale

INTRODUCTION

That there has long been in the United States a working class numbering in the millions, with needs and interests of its own;

that significant aspects of the experience and culture of these workers set them apart, even if not quite so sharply as in Europe, from other social classes;

that many American workers have organized themselves into trade unions which together comprise a powerful labor movement, defending the rights of its members and often acting in behalf of social betterment throughout the nation—

all of these may seem utterly self-evident statements, indeed, self-evident to the point of the commonplace.

But they are not.

For the truth is that the working class, both as actuality and idea, has never been wholly accepted in American society or adequately reflected in American culture. My own recollections from school and college are that trade unions or the workers as a distinct social group were rarely mentioned in classrooms or textbooks. If you look at our popular culture—from comic strips to movies, from novels to television—you will be struck by the extent to which this crucial segment of the American people is blocked out. A film like *Norma Rae* comes to seem notable simply because it is there.

Why should this be so? One reason, I think, is that a recognition of the working class as a major component of American society runs counter to the dominant American myth. That is a myth of a nation of independent craftsmen, small farmers, sturdy businessmen, usually self-employed, sometimes hiring a few "hands," but mostly succeeding through their own industriousness and sobriety. It is a myth closer to the realities of the age of Jefferson, even Andrew Jackson, than the age of Nixon and Carter.

The persistence of this myth in American life is something to marvel at. It fails increasingly to describe our social reality, yet it hangs on. It is utterly inadequate to—indeed, glaringly in contradiction with—the America of giant industries, massive plants, concentrated wealth, enormous multinational corporations. But people want it, need it.

That this myth once had great liberating power in our society and culture; that it still has some attractive moral elements, such as a stress on individual effort and a defense of private life—yes, of course. But in its decline from Ralph Waldo Emerson to Herbert Hoover (and all the mini-Hoovers of later years), it has often disabled us from seeing what is there in front of our collective nose.

And still, we cling to that myth. We cling to its picture of a small-town or pastoral nation, if only because it answers some deep need within us, some overpowering nostalgia. Perhaps it's a case of what historians call "cultural lag," sentiment and idea lagging behind reality. Sometimes this lagging can even serve a useful purpose: it may enable keen criticisms of our social arrangements. Sometimes, I would say more often, this myth is cynically exploited, as in political ballyhoo and corporate advertising. Anti-union corporations appeal to the tradition of "individualism"—as if a solitary worker, unlinked with the workers next to him, could ever be a match for the wealth and power of a giant company!

One reason for the reluctance to acknowledge the sheer idea of an American working class has been the claim—and it has some truth to it—that things in America are "different." American workers, it is said, are not so rigidly held into fixed or limited class positions as workers in Europe. That may also explain why the American labor movement has not been nearly so friendly to socialist ideas as the European labor movement. And as I say, there is some truth to these claims, though with the passage of time, less and less truth. Mainly, however, the idea of the working class as a distinct and major presence in American life has not been fully accepted because of our incorrigible nostalgia for an earlier, simpler America where there were few industrial laborers, few large corporations, few immense cities.

But there is no going back. Whatever else, for good or bad, we cannot go back to this earlier America. It no longer exists, except in isolated pockets here and there. We will either work our way to a more democratically humane and socially just society within the context of advanced industrialism, or we will drift further into a corporate-dominated, bureaucratically-managed society. In either case, however, advanced industrialism (or post-industrialism) will remain, and so too will a significant working class and strong labor movement.

What seems especially strange about these failures in national self-perception is that work as human activity finds a very important place in 19th century American literature. In Whitman's poems work is lyrically celebrated; in Mark Twain's *Life on the Mississippi* work is lovingly evoked; in Herman Melville's *Moby Dick* work is described with a passion for exact detail. For the most part, however, the work portrayed in 19th century American literature is that of the independent craftsman—the steamboatman of Twain, the day printer of Whitman. And the same seems to be true for 19th century American painting.

The worker as we know him and her first appears in a strange, haunting story by Melville, "The Paradise of Bachelors and the Tartarus of Maids." Set in a 19th century factory, this story anticipates the work that we know in factories and shops: the dehumanized labor of men and women tending machines. "At rows of blank-looking counters sat rows of blank-looking girls, with blank, white folders in their blank hands, all blankly folding blank paper.... The human voice was banished from the spot. Machinery—that vaunted slave of humanity—here stood menially served by human beings, who served mutely and clingingly as the slave serves the Sultan."

This anticipation—eerie, moving—of modern factory life is notable for its rarity. Only with Theodore Dreiser's great novel, *Sister Carrie*, in which a young farm girl suddenly finds herself laboring in a Chicago shoe factory, do we fully confront the modern industrial world. Dreiser offers a grueling description of the tediousness and exhaustion of factory labor: "Her hands began to ache at the wrists and then in the fingers, and toward the last she seemed one mass of dull, complaining muscles, fixed in an eternal position, and performing a single mechanical movement...."

Such recognitions are not the rule. It is easier to slip into the cliches of "individualist" nostalgia and bland denial, ignoring the reality of the American workers, pretending they have little or no shared existence. But to block out of our national consciousness the lives of millions upon millions of human beings is a form of snobbery. It is reactionary. It is inhumane.

Once American society entered the era of industrial urbanism in the last third of the 19th century, it underwent a major change in social structure. The dynamic of capitalist development brought a greater concentration of economic power. Now, most workers were employed by an impersonal company or corporation. Populations were reshuffled. Millions left the small towns and farms. The craftsman faded from the scene. Lifestyles were adapted to the stringent demands of the factory. No longer—except in a few "light" industries like those manufacturing women's garments—could work be located in the home or done by the family. The lure of business profits led to large-scale manufacturing away from home, outside the family, cut off from familiar community, beyond any previously-known structure of work.

More and more, the factory came to be an institution antithetical to humane values. No longer was "sweat" a metaphor for the satisfying reward of a day's toil. Instead it meant work in airless lofts that were often incubators of disease, or on assembly lines with no safety standards. Wages were often as close to subsistence as employers could get away with.

It's roughly at this historical moment, in the latter half of the 19th century, that large-scale unionism was born. There had of course been unions before then, heroic and combative ones earlier in the century. But now, driven by need into the vast new complexes of city and factory, and often consisting of immigrants still confused by their new circumstances in America, the workers began to organize in self-defense.

It was hard. Blood was shed and repressive legislation enacted. Brutal injunctions were issued by union-busting judges. The early years of the American labor movement form a desperate time, not nearly well-enough known. It is a time of violent struggle, of strikes kept going through struggle and defeat, of a society still largely operating with the laws of the jungle, a crude notion of "survival of the fittest."

Even in these early, difficult years, the labor movement stressed more than hours and wages, desperately urgent as hours and wages were to millions of people. This country could not have survived as a democracy if its working people had not enforced the claims and enlarged the scope of democracy by organizing in protection of their rights. You can always measure the level of democracy in any country by the freedom its workers have to organize unions of their own choosing. But more: the unions struggled for some larger vision of fraternity and decency. They were among the major social groups that campaigned for free, universal public education. They imbued their members with a sense of dignity, the persuasion that they were not just numbered cogs in someone else's machine.

Let's go back a bit, say a hundred years. One of the big issues then was the ten-hour day. In New Hampshire, for instance, the legislature limited the working day to ten hours unless the worker chose to work more, while children under fifteen could not work more than ten hours under any conditions. (Which tells you something about child labor.) Women in Oregon waited until 1903 before legislation limited their working day to ten hours. Later in this book you'll read the testimony of Frances Perkins, Secretary of Labor under President Franklin Roosevelt, about women and children working long hours in abysmal conditions in upstate New York canneries well into this century. Does anyone with eyes to see and ears to hear suppose that all of these shameful conditions have been ended in America?

In 1912 mill hands in the textile factories of Lawrence, Massachusetts were earning about as much as their forebears had earned a hundred years earlier—an average weekly wage of $8.76 which in slack times could fall below $3. When the Massachusetts legislature reduced working hours for women and children under eighteen from fifty-six to fifty-four hours, the mill owners obliged, but also reduced wages by a like amount. It enraged the mill hands, who walked off the job. By the next day, and without the organizing skills of a union, angry workers shut all the mills in Lawrence. This became one of the great labor struggles in the United States. Instinctively the strikers turned to an all-industry industrial structure, as against separation by craft. They organized relief, sent children to live with relatives beyond the strike zone. Liberals and reformers provided some money for help. The strike 'for Bread and Roses' was won, with wage increases of five to twenty-five percent that soon were extended to more than 200,000 textile workers throughout New England.

There have been hundreds, thousands of other such battles. It turned out that you had to keep fighting all the time, in defense of rights already won, on behalf of improvements long overdue. There was no resting. Unions that fell back on their haunches were soon unions without members, without achievements. Because no matter how much employers and their spokesmen sweet-talked, they were always ready to take the initiative, begin a counter-attack.

Efforts were made to form a national federation of unions: some failed because the times were not yet ripe and the opposition was too fierce, but later, others succeeded. The National Labor Union, organized in 1866, had the splendid idea of rejecting within its ranks all distinctions of race or nationality. "We are all," said its head William Sylvis, "one family of slaves together. The labor movement is a second Emancipation Proclamation." That's about as far as it went, though the President of the Colored National Labor Union, formed just after the Civil War, was seated as a delegate to a NLU convention. When the feminists of the day threatened to scab unless admitted as equals to the union, the delegates grew antagonistic. How much more sensible it would have been to "sign them up" on the spot!

The National Labor Union didn't last long, but it paved the way, and then came a more significant national body, the Knights of Labor, which by the 1880's had close to a million members. A mixture of lodge and union, the Knights practiced all sorts of secret rituals, partly for the fun of it, partly to protect themselves from informers. Flourishing for a time and then declining, the Knights were replaced in 1886 by the American Federation of Labor, the most stable grouping of American unions we've ever had. Even in its youthful fragility, the AFL made a mark by campaigning, under Samuel Gompers' shrewd pragmatic leadership, for the eight-hour day. In language more conservative than earlier unions, though in practice often fighting bitter battles, the AFL usually avoided political and ideological issues and concentrated on "bread and butter." Bread being expensive and butter scarce, this strategy often worked. The AFL became the umbrella group for a number of strong craft unions made up mostly of skilled workers; but millions of industrial workers, supposedly "unorganizable," were ignored. They had to wait till the early 1930's, when the CIO was formed under the colorful leadership of John L. Lewis, the head of the miners' union. Spurred by the wretched circumstances of the Depression years, enabled partly by New Deal legislation, and often staffed by idealistic young radicals, the CIO swept through the country organizing auto, steel, chemicals, rubber, and a bit later hospital and municipal employees. It was an exciting moment—I remember it from my own early adolescence—when hundreds of thousands of workers poured into the unions, went out on sit-down strikes, suddenly showed remarkable gifts of organization and capacities for sacrifice. In 1955 the AFL and CIO came together in one federation.

Strong though it remains, the AFL-CIO still represents only about a fifth of the American working class. Major gains have been made since the days of Franklin Roosevelt and John L. Lewis—don't let anyone tell you otherwise! The "welfare state"—which means a society that doesn't trust to the magical "laws of the market" but intervenes actively in behalf of the poor and helpless—is still very far from what it should be. But the lives of millions of workers are now far better than they were several decades ago. We have old age pensions, social security, unemployment insurance, and above all, the right to organize. Even when some hard-bitten corporations tried, in the late 1970's, to bust unions, they had to go against the more-or-less established norms of the society; in the late 1920's, it was the exact opposite.

Let's be candid. Trade unions are led by men and women, not saints; their membership consists of fallible human beings, not ideal "proletarians." This is to say that trade unions have their faults. Some are very far from what they should be with regard to internal democracy; the record concerning treatment of opposition and dissident groups is spotty. Other unions are hidebound, rigid, and unconcerned with anything but the immediate needs of their members. (Not that there is anything wrong with being concerned with immediate needs!) Still other unions have until recently discriminated against blacks—I'm pretty sure that while there have been major improvements in this respect, there is still room for more. And only recently have unions begun to show an appropriate sensitivity to the demands and needs of women.

The prejudices of our society and the corruptions of our culture, necessarily seep into the unions. It could hardly be otherwise, but this makes them a target for criticism. Some of that criticism is valid, some not.

I've already indicated kinds of criticism that seem sensible, but here let me mention two kinds that do not. The first kind comes from sectarian "leftists" who complain that unions collaborate with employers (but they *have* to sign contracts, they *have* to work within the limits of the given situation, even if they are also trying to extend those limits). That unions don't take the lead in making revolutions is entirely understandable, since they aren't organized for that purpose—they are organized to protect the interests of all workers, both the vast majority who don't want revolutions and the tiny minority who say they do. The other kind of criticism comes from high-minded middle-class folk who, from some perch of rectitude, complain that unions aren't sufficiently concerned with "the general welfare." Let's acknowledge that sometimes this is true. But more often, it is nonsense. For when unions fight for minimum wage laws or regulations providing safety on the job, they are protecting millions upon millions of people, including many who are not even union members. There's a tendency in American discourse to talk about some abstract "public," but in fact the actual public contains a very large segment of working people. When I read an editorial or hear a speech counterposing the "public" to the unions, I grow suspicious.

I come from the generation that entered early adolescence just as this country was succumbing to the Great Depression. The desperation, the poverty, the sheer sense of helplessness of those days forms an experience almost impossible to communicate to younger people lucky enough not to have known it firsthand.

My parents had to find jobs in the garment industry once their little store went bankrupt in 1931. I remember my mother coming home exhausted each evening, and ending the week with a $12 paycheck. I remember my father, who stood all day over a steaming press-iron, coming home during the summer months with blisters all over his body. When the great strike of the garment workers was called by the International Ladies Garment Workers Union in 1933, my folks, who had had no experience with unions before, responded immediately. Like tens of thousands of others, they picketed, they borrowed money for food, they stood fast. The strike over, my mother brought home her first new paycheck: $27. It seemed like heaven: we felt freer, better, stronger. And there was meat on the table. After that, my folks were never active in the union, but they paid their dues faithfully, and if a strike was called, they were the first to go out. This was the ethic I grew up with, the ethic of solidarity. Almost half a century later, I still believe in it.

So when I hear snobs and reactionaries attack unions, I find myself going into a rage. Sure, I know the unions are open to criticism on many counts; but I continue to believe that without them our lives would be far worse than they are. I know for certain that mine would have been far worse.

The unions form a backbone of social strength; they make life a little better for the underpaid, the oppressed; I want them to improve but I want them to grow stronger too.

It is time we recognized, in our social arrangements and our cultural experience, the centrality of the American working class. Much of what passes among us for immigrant history, as well as the history of minority groups, really has to do with the working class. If we don't within the working class of this country have as cohesive and visible a "common culture" as has existed in Europe, that is partly due to the diversity, the newness, the sheer size of America. But dig a little beneath the surface, brush aside the conventional myths and cliches of American middle-class life, and you will find plenty of evidence that workers and their unions ought to be far more prominent in our cultural expression than they are. Not in any crude propagandistic sense, but with sympathetic and critical honesty. Perhaps this book will take us a step in that direction.

—*Irving Howe*

Man is born to Labor and the bird to fly.

—Job v 7

Painting by Paul Davis

© 1980 Paul Davis

Look at me! Look at my arm!
I have ploughed and planted. And
ain't I a woman? I could work
as much and eat as much as a man—
when I could get it—and bear the
lash as well—And ain't I a woman?
                              —Sojourner Truth

Painting by Audrey Flack

Power concedes nothing without a demand. It never did, and it never will. Find out just what people will submit to and you have found out the exact amount of injustice and wrong which will be imposed upon them; and these will continue till they have resisted with either words or blows, or with both. The limits of tyrants are prescribed by the endurance of those whom they suppress.   *—Frederick Douglass*

Painting by Robert Weaver

The labor movement is about that problem we face tomorrow morning. Damn right! But to make that the sole purpose of the labor movement is to miss the main target. I mean, 'What good is a dollar an hour more in wages if your neighborhood is burning down? What good is another week's vacation if the lake you used to go to is polluted and you can't swim in it and the kids can't play in it? What good is another $100 pension if the world goes up in atomic smoke?'

—*Walter P. Reuther*

Construction by Mimi Gross

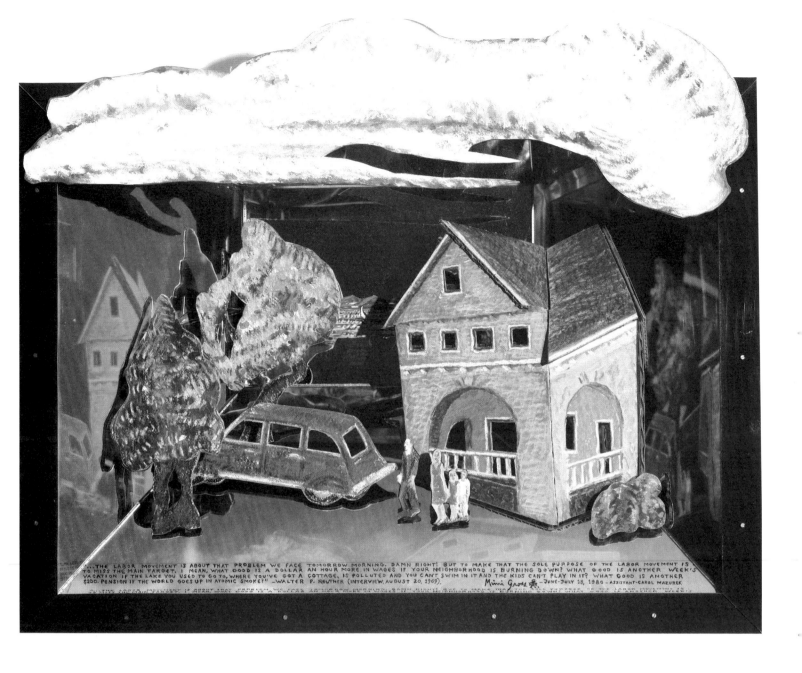

"...THE LABOR MOVEMENT IS ABOUT THAT PROBLEM WE FACE TOMORROW MORNING. DAMN RIGHT! BUT TO MAKE THAT THE SOLE PURPOSE OF THE LABOR MOVEMENT IS TO MISS THE MAIN TARGET, I MEAN, WHAT GOOD IS A DOLLAR AN HOUR MORE IN WAGES IF YOUR NEIGHBORHOOD IS BURNING DOWN? WHAT GOOD IS ANOTHER WEEK'S VACATION IF THE LAKE YOU USED TO GO TO, WHERE YOU'VE GOT A COTTAGE, IS POLLUTED AND YOU CAN'T SWIM IN IT AND THE KIDS CAN'T PLAY IN IT? WHAT GOOD IS ANOTHER $100. PENSION IF THE WORLD GOES UP IN ATOMIC SMOKE?" —WALTER P. REUTHER (INTERVIEW, AUGUST 20, 1969)

Mimi Gross — JUNE-JULY 18, 1980 — ASSISTANT-CAROL MAZUREK

Goodbye Bill:
I die like a true rebel. Don't waste
any time mourning—organize! It
is a hundred miles from here to
Wyoming. Could you arrange to
have my body hauled to the state
line to be buried? I don't want to be
found dead in Utah.   *—Joe Hill*

Painting by James McMullan

Women, as well as men, were given minds to use and the ability to develop skills in various ways. I believe this is so primarily because, in the scheme of the universe, for real satisfaction every human being must earn his living. If you have gifts, natural gifts, and you never develop them, you are as guilty as the man in the Bible who wrapped his talent in a napkin and buried it so he could return to his Master what his Master had given him.

—Eleanor Roosevelt

Cut Paper by Jacqueline Chwast

We still have those who believe in the archaic traditions of the 1880s and 1890s; those who believe that America is built from the top down, that if you keep the great corporations fat and wealthy, enough will trickle down to keep those at the lower level of our economic structure happy and contented.   —*George Meany*

Painting by Honoré Sharrer

So long as there is one man who seeks employment and cannot obtain it, the hours of work are too long.

—*Samuel Gompers*

Ceramic Mask by Robert Arneson

Now some people say a man's
   made out of mud,
But a poor man's made out of
   muscle and blood,
Muscle and blood, skin and bone,
A mind that's weak and a back
   that's strong.
You load sixteen tons and what do
   you get?
You get another day older and
   deeper in debt.
Saint Peter, don't you call me 'cause
   I can't go,
I owe my soul to the company store.

                 —Merle Travis
                 "Sixteen Tons"

Painting by Robert Grossman

We are the slaves of slaves. We are exploited more ruthlessly than men.
—*Lucy Parsons*

Painting by May Stevens

slaves of slaves. We are exploited more ruthlessly than men.

Lucy E. Parsons
1905

It is true, indeed, that they can execute the body, but they cannot execute the idea which is bound to live.   —*Nicola Sacco*

Painting by Milton Glaser

We weave the flag.
We live under the flag.
We die under the flag.
But damn'd if we'll starve
    under the flag.
    —Paterson Silk Strike banner, 1913

Painting by Barbara Nessim

© Barbara Nessim · 1980

The strongest bond of human
sympathy, outside of the
family relation, should be one uniting
all working people, of all nations,
and tongues, and kindreds.

—Abraham Lincoln

Sculpture by William King

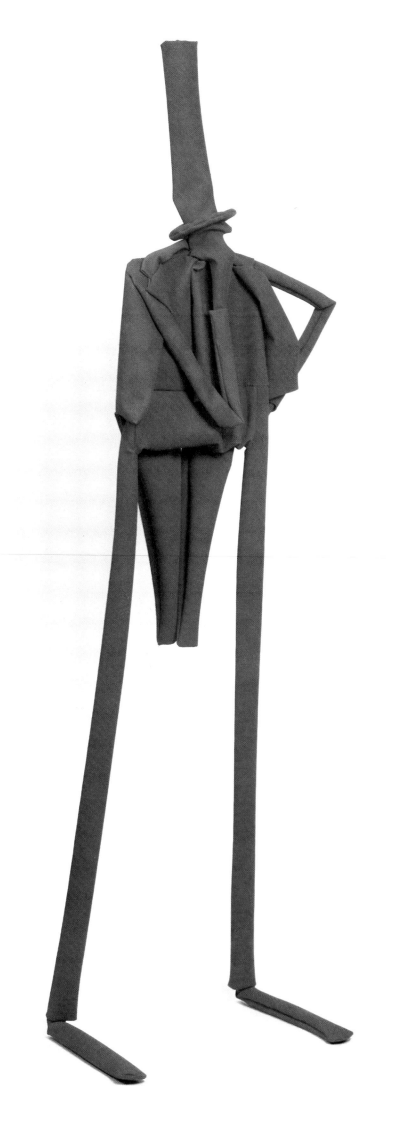

An injury to one is an injury to all.
—Knights of Labor motto

Painting by Daniel Maffia

They take the paper and they read
  the headlines,
So they've heard of unemployment
  and they've heard of breadlines,
And they philanthropically cure
  them all
By getting up a costume charity
  ball.

—Ogden Nash
"Pride Goeth Before a Raise"

Drawing by Seymour Chwast

We were nervous and we didn't know we could do it. Those machines had kept going as long as we could remember. When we finally pulled the switch and there was some quiet, I finally remembered something…that I was a human being, that I could stop those machines, that I was *better* than those machines anytime.

—Sit-down striker
Akron, Ohio 1936

Painting by Sue Coe

They don't suffer; they can't even
speak English.　　　　*—George Baer*

Drawing by Edward Sorel

Boys picking slate in a coal breaker in Anthracite Mines, Pennsylvania

Alfred E. Smith and Robert Wagner, who later became great leaders in social justice, got their education as members of the Factory Investigation Commission. I was an investigator for the Commission. We made sure that Robert Wagner personally crawled through the tiny hole in the wall that gave egress to a steep iron ladder covered with ice and ending twelve feet from the ground, which was euphemistically labeled "Fire Escape" in many factories. We saw to it that the austere legislative members of the Commission got up at dawn and drove with us for an unannounced visit to a Cattaraugus County cannery and that they saw with their own eyes the little children, not adolescents, but five-, six-, and seven-year-olds, snipping beans and shelling peas. We made sure that they saw the machinery that would scalp a girl or cut off a man's arm. Hours so long that both men and women were depleted and exhausted became realities to them through seeing for themselves the dirty little factories.

—Frances Perkins

Painting by Alice Neel

Our lives shall not be sweated
from birth until life closes,
hearts starve as well as bodies; give
us bread, but give us roses!
—James Oppenheim
"Bread and Roses"

Drawing by Jack Beal

In 1931 and 1932 I went into towns where children were eating out of garbage pails. People were living in hovels. No pictures on the walls, no carpets on the floors, no music in the homes. The working population was suffering and in too many instances was starving. Disease, sickness and poverty were rampant, and death stalked in the wake of every worker's family because he could not purchase medicine.   —*Philip Murray*

Painting by Ralph Fasanella

The essence of trade unionism is social uplift. The labor movement traditionally has been the haven for the dispossessed, the despised, the neglected, the downtrodden, the poor. *—A. Philip Randolph*

Painting by Marshall Arisman

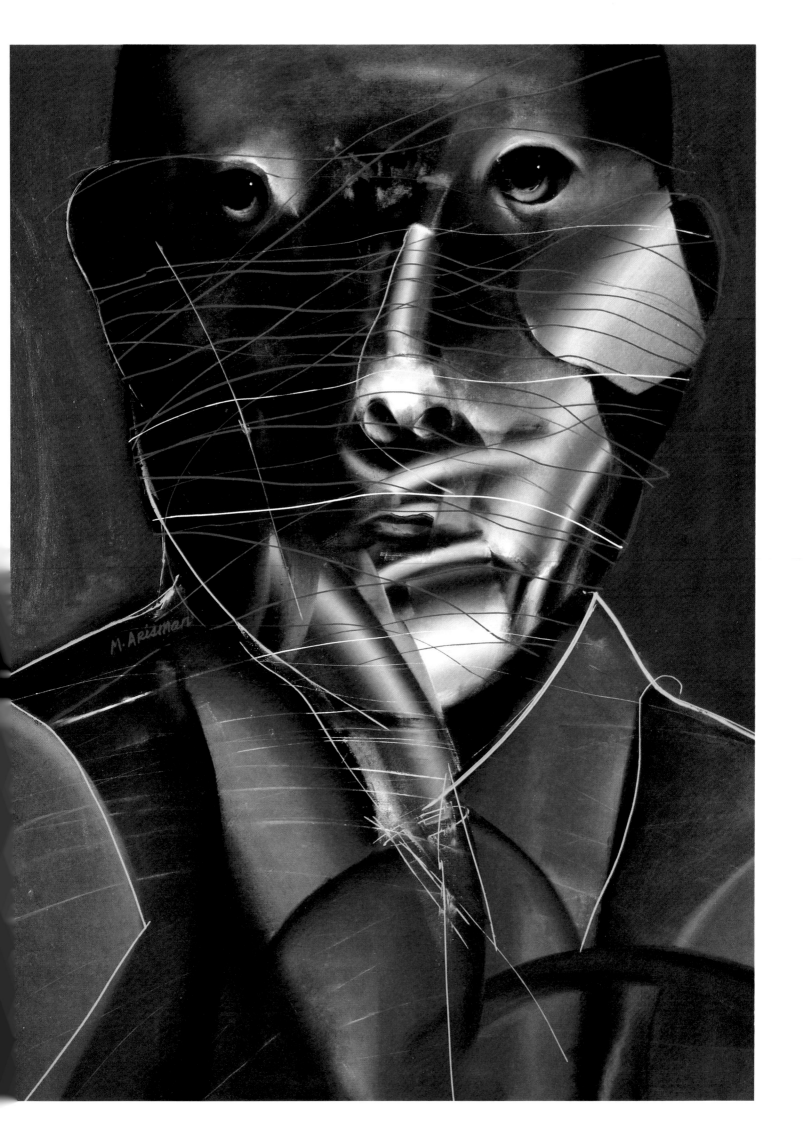

This is not the first time girls have been burned alive in this city. Every week I must learn of the untimely death of one of my sister workers. Every year thousands of us are maimed. The life of men and women is so cheap and property is so sacred! —*Rose Schneiderman*

Drawing by Judy Chicago

The coal operators would think they got the union crushed, but just like putting out a fire, you can go out and stomp on it and leave a few sparks and here come a wind and it's going to spread again. —*Hobert Grills*

Painting by Benny Andrews

You may call the workers' phrases vulgar and untrained, but to me their forms of speech are much more clear, more powerful, with more courage and poetry than all your schools in which our leaders smile to see us learn empty grammar. A man's most basic character, most basic wants, hopes and needs come out of him in words that are poems and explosions.   —*Woody Guthrie*

Painting by Philip Hays

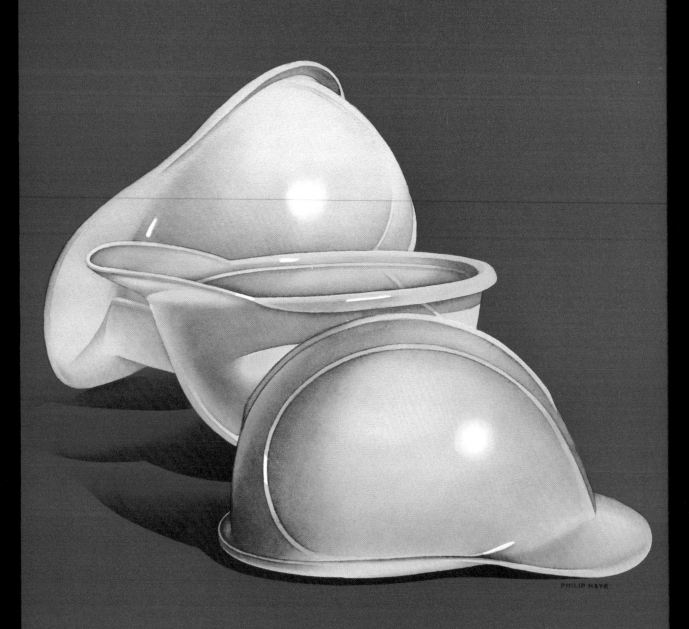

The open shop is a harlot with a wig and artificial limbs and her bones rattle. —*John L. Lewis*

Painting by Anton van Dalen

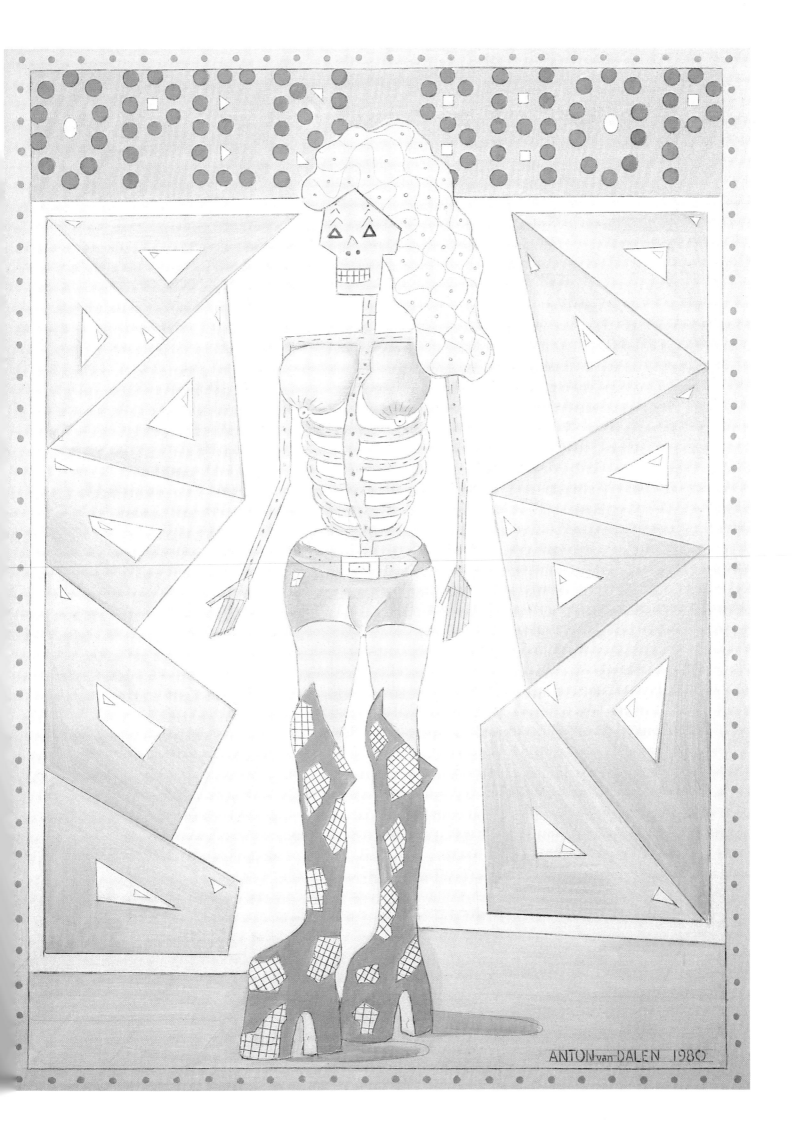

ANTON van DALEN 1980

When people have melons or cucumbers or carrots or lettuce, they don't know how they got on their table, and the consequences to the people who picked them. If I had enough money, I would take busloads of people out to the fields and into the labor camps. Then they'd know how that fine salad got on their table.   *—Roberto Acuna*
Farm worker

Construction by Miriam Wosk

The labor-hater and labor-baiter is virtually always a twinheaded creature spewing anti-Negro epithets from one mouth and anti-labor propaganda from the other mouth.   *—Martin Luther King, Jr.*

Painting by Brad Holland

Intelligent discontent is the mainspring of civilization. Progress is born of agitation. It is agitation or stagnation. —*Eugene V. Debs*

Collage by Anita Siegel

I live in the United States, but I do not know exactly where. My address is wherever there is a fight against oppression. My address is like my shoes; it travels with me. I abide where there is a fight against wrong. —*Mother Jones*

Sculpture by Ed McGowin

INTERIOR

Who are the oppressors? The few: the king, the capitalist, and a handful of other overseers and superintendents. Who are the oppressed? The many: the nations of the earth, the valuable personages, the workers; they that *make* the bread that the soft-handed and idle eat. *—Mark Twain*

Painting by Jacob Lawrence

You never come back.
I say goodbye when I see you going
  in the doors,
The hopeless open doors that call
  and wait
And take you then for—how many
  cents a day?
How many cents for the sleepy eyes
  and fingers?   *—Carl Sandburg*
                    "Mill Doors"

Drawing by John Collier

The mass of mankind has not been born with saddles on their backs, nor a favored few booted and spurred.   *—Thomas Jefferson*

Drawing by Luis Jimenez, Jr.

SOURCES

ROBERTO ACUNA, FARM WORKER

Source: Studs Terkel, *Working*, (New York: Avon Books, 1972), p. 38.

Roberto Acuna became an organizer for the United Farm Workers because he saw the need to change the "California feudal system," to improve the lives of the Mexican-American farm workers, and to make the growers realize that they weren't "above anybody." In an effort to bring the growers to the bargaining table, the union launched a national boycott campaign in the mid-1960s to publicize the plight of the farm workers and to ensure that American consumers did not buy non-union produce. Despite the success of the campaign, many Americans remain completely ignorant of the farm workers' struggle for justice. Thus Acuna's desire to "take bus-loads of people out to the fields and into the labor camps."

AKRON SIT-DOWN STRIKER

Source: *URW-25: A Quarter Century Panorama of Democratic Unionism,* (Akron: United Rubber Workers, AFL-CIO, 1960).

Since the beginning of the industrial revolution, labor-saving and skill-reducing machinery has rendered manual labor speedy and monotonous. By the 1930s, most workers in mass production industries had become little more than robots. In response to the speed-up, unsafe working conditions, low pay and lack of job security, rubber workers in Akron, Ohio developed a tactic which was completely new to American industrial disputes: the sit-down strike.

Between 1933 and 1936, sit-downs became something of a tradition in Akron. Always disciplined, the strikers not only spontaneously shut down production, but made it impossible for the companies to hire strikebreakers. Moreover, as a result of their ability to stop production, many workers realized for the first time that they could control rubber tire production.

Employers, to a man, considered the sit-downs a violation of the rights of private property; in short, a form of socialism. But the strikers' aims were far less prodigious: they sat down to protest their exploitation and used the tactic to bring the rubber companies to the bargaining table.

GEORGE BAER (1824-1914)

Source: Elizabeth Levy and Tad Richards, *Struggle and Lose, Struggle and Win: The United Mine Workers of America,* (New York: Four Winds Press, 1977), p. 27.

In 1902, the United Mine Workers of America declared a strike which idled 150,000 Polish, Hungarian, Lithuanian, Ukranian and Romanian immigrant miners in north-eastern Pennsylvania. The anthracite miners demanded shorter hours, higher wages and union recognition. The coal operators saw these demands as threats to their managerial prerogatives and refused to meet with the union. Of all the operators, George Baer, the President of the Philadelphia and Reading Railroad, was the most virulently anti-union. In addition to his remark that the strikers "don't suffer" because "they can't even speak English," Baer insisted that "the rights and interests of the laboring man will be protected and cared for not by the labor agitators, but by the Christian men to whom God in His infinite wisdom has given the control of the property interests of the Country...." Expressions of arrogance and obstinance such as these arrayed public opinion against the operators and encouraged President Theodore Roosevelt to appoint a Commission to help arbitrate the dispute. Although it did not grant the union formal recognition, the Commission did set a precedent for collective bargaining between the union and the operators.

EUGENE V. DEBS (1855-1926)

Source: George Seldes, *The Great Quotations*, (New York: Lyle-Stuart, 1960), p. 197.

Eugene V. Debs is without question the foremost socialist political leader in the history of American radicalism. Dissatisfied with the conservative craft brotherhoods which organized only skilled railroad workers, Debs, a Secretary of the Brotherhood of Locomotive Firemen, began organizing the American Railway Union in 1892—an industrial union which represented all workers regardless of skill. Despite early success, the union was broken by the Federal government during the Pullman boycott of 1894, and Debs was jailed for six months for conspiring to obstruct the delivery of Federal mail. In prison, Debs became a socialist.

Drawing on Biblical imagery, the republicanism of Thomas Paine, the utopianism of Edward Bellamy, and the writings of Karl Marx, Debs fashioned a socialist vision which many workers found compelling. Although his Socialist Party never became a truly mass party, Debs polled nearly one million votes as Presidential candidate in 1912. A lifelong crusader for the "cooperative commonwealth," Debs was the only radical in American history to create a large, national working class socialist constituency.

FREDERICK DOUGLASS (1817-1895)

Source: Philip Foner, *Frederick Douglass, A Biography*, (New York: Citadel Press, 1964), p. 11.

A black abolitionist, orator and journalist, Frederick Douglass escaped from slavery in 1838 and eventually settled in New England where, after reading William Garrison's abolitionist newspaper, *The Liberator*, he became a leader of the Massachusetts anti-slavery movement. An imposing figure and an eloquent speaker, Douglass denounced slavery from firsthand knowledge. In 1848 he began publishing his own newspaper, *The Northern Star*, through which he advocated not only the abolition of slavery but women's rights.

For Douglass, human liberty could only be achieved through moral and physical force. He urged black people both free and slave to rise up against the slave owners, and during the Civil War, continually urged Abraham Lincoln to transform the Union Army into an army of liberation.

SAMUEL GOMPERS (1850-1924)

Source: Second Annual Convention of the American Federation of Labor, *Report of the Proceedings*, Baltimore, Maryland, December 13, 1887, p. 9.

Of all American labor leaders, Samuel Gompers had the greatest impact on the political character of the modern American labor movement. A cigarmaker by trade, Gompers flirted with socialism as a young man, but after 1886 increasingly eschewed radical political solutions in favor of "business unionism." For Gompers, the interests of laboring men and women could best be served by craft unions of skilled workers which would fight for shorter hours, higher wages and better working conditions. Accepting the capitalist system as a given, Gompers and other craft unionists formed the American Federation of Labor in 1886. As President of the AFL between 1886 and 1924, Gompers was severely criticized by William D. Haywood of the Industrial Workers of the World and Eugene V. Debs of the Socialist Party. Despite these criticisms from the left, the AFL remained the largest and most stable organization of American workers.

HOBERT GRILLS

Source: Bill Bishop, "1931: The Battle of Evarts," *Southern Exposure*, 4 (1976), p. 92.

From 1931 to the present, Harlan County, Kentucky has been the scene of the bloodiest and most bitterly fought struggles in American labor history. Despite the powerful armed resistance of the coal companies, the Harlan County miners have continued to fight for the right to belong to trade unions and to have that union recognized by the companies.

Although the County has not yet been fully organized, the legacy of the Harlan County labor wars is not one of defeat. As Hobert Grills, a veteran coal miner who took part in the 1931 strike, reminds us, the true legacy is the spirit of resistance which will one day burst into a new and more volatile flame.

WOODY GUTHRIE (1912-1967)

Source: Woody Guthrie in a letter to his wife, Marjorie, December 1945 while serving in the U.S. Air Force in Las Vegas, Nevada.

Born in Okemah, Oklahoma, Woody Guthrie has become a legend in the annals of American folk music. His songs and ballads such as "This Land Is Your Land," "Union Maid," "So Long, It's Been Good to Know You," and countless others, reflect the experiences and outlook of the rural and urban poor, particularly those buffeted by the Dust Bowl and the Great Depression of the 1930s. An inheritor of the southwestern populist/socialist tradition, many of Guthrie's songs question the primacy of private property over human rights.

JOE HILL (1879-1915)

Source: Philip S. Foner, (ed.), *The Letters of Joe Hill*, (New York: Oak Publications, 1965), p. 84.

America has a rich tradition of labor songs, many of them written by the Swedish immigrant Joe Hill. Working as a harvester, copper miner, and seaman, Hill became interested in radical trade unionism and joined the San Pedro, California chapter of the Industrial Workers of the World (IWW), a revolutionary socialist organization which organized exploited and unskilled workers who were ignored by the AFL. Hill's songs were intended to "fan the flames of discontent" amongst itinerant agricultural workers, timber workers, unskilled eastern and southern European immigrants, and racially excluded blacks, Mexicans and Asians, and bolstered their solidarity on picket lines and in prison cells.

Hill's career as the "Wobblies" premier "troubador of discontent" was cut short when he was arrested and indicted for the murder of a Salt Lake City grocer. Although some circumstantial evidence indicated his guilt, the prosecution was never able to obtain proof. Despite massive demonstrations on his behalf, he was executed by a firing squad in the Utah State Prison on November 19, 1915. On the day before his execution, Hill wrote "Wobbly" leader "Big Bill" Haywood imploring him not to mourn for his death, but to organize.

THOMAS JEFFERSON (1743-1826)
Letter to Roger C. Weightman, June 24, 1826

Source: Adrienne Koch (ed.), *Jefferson—Great Lives Observed*, (Englewood Cliffs: Prentice Hall, 1971), p. 81.

The author of the Declaration of Independence and the third President of the United States, Jefferson's thought was greatly influenced by the Enlightenment of the eighteenth century. From this intellectual revolution, he drew the conclusion that all men were created equal and had a natural right to self-government. Despite his egalitarianism, Jefferson was no social leveller: he believed that a "natural aristocracy" chosen by an independent and educated class of yeoman farmers could best conduct the affairs of the new nation. Nevertheless, his political philosophy marked a sharp departure from elitist ideas concerning government, and his writing has endured as an inspiration to leaders of democratic mass movements for social change.

JOB 5:7

A statement by Eliphaz the Temanite in the book of Job in the Old Testament

MARTIN LUTHER KING, JR. (1929-1968)

Source: M.B. Schnapper, *American Labor, A Bicentennial History*, (Washington, D.C.: Public Affairs Press, 1975), p. 556.

In addition to his leadership of the Civil Rights movement of the 1950s and '60s, Martin Luther King, Jr. was also a strong supporter of the trade union movement. In his struggle against white racism, King learned that the enemies of black civil rights were often extremely hostile to the labor movement. Since most blacks were wage earners, and since trade unions were vehicles of social justice and equality, King in his later life became an earnest crusader for labor, particularly municipal and hospital workers. At the time of his assassination, King was leading a strike of Memphis, Tennessee sanitation workers.

KNIGHTS OF LABOR

Source: Seldes, *The Great Quotations*, p. 392.

Unlike the craft-oriented American Federation of Labor, the Knights of Labor organized all workers regardless of sex, race, or skill. Beginning in 1869 as a secret society, the Knights experienced an enormous period of national growth, from 19,000 in 1881 to 111,000 in 1885.

Both visionary and pragmatic, the Knights maintained a vision of a harmonious society in which class distinctions would be erased through the establishment of producer and consumer cooperatives, and advocated the immediate establishment of boards of arbitration, the eight-hour day, health and safety legislation and other reforms.

Internal conflict and an employers' counter-offensive took its toll on the Knights and they declined rapidly after 1887. Nevertheless they left a legacy of industrial unionism and working class solidarity which was best expressed in their motto.

JOHN L. LEWIS (1880-1961)

President of the United Mine Workers of America, and founder of the CIO, John L. Lewis played a leading role in the great organizing drives of the 1930s which established trade unions amongst unskilled mass production workers. His spirited leadership, the militancy of the rank and file, and the legitimizing effect of New Deal labor legislation combined to win collective bargaining agreements from such traditionally open-shop companies as U.S. Steel, Goodyear Tire and Rubber, and General Motors. These contracts transformed the nature of American industrial relations and began a new era in American trade unionism.

ABRAHAM LINCOLN (1809-1865)
Reply to a Committee from The New York Workingmen's Association, March 21, 1864

Abraham Lincoln was a believer in self-government—the idea that people are able to govern themselves. He worked to ensure freedom of opinion and speech, and appointed both conservatives and radicals to his cabinet toward that end. As a self-made man, he believed that sober, frugal, and hardworking people could achieve upward mobility, and advocated that government provide an equal opportunity for all people, regardless of race, to acquire wealth and property.

GEORGE MEANY (1894-1980)
Acceptance Speech at the December 1955 Merger Convention of the AFL-CIO

Source: *American Federationist* 63 (January 1956), p. 15.

Between 1935 and 1955, two labor movements existed in America: the AFL which organized skilled workers along craft lines, and the CIO which organized unskilled workers into industrial unions. Although a bitter rivalry existed between the two during the Great Depression, the passage of anti-labor legislation such as the Taft/Hartley Act brought the two organizations together in 1955.

At the Merger Convention, George Meany, a plumber by trade and President of the AFL from 1952 to 1979, enumerated the benefits of a united labor movement and emphasized the need to organize the unorganized. The bulk of Meany's speech, however, was concerned with the Taft/Hartley Act—a piece of legislation which he believed negated the pro-labor legislation of the New Deal years, and returned the labor movement to a time when trade unions had no legal right to organize.

MOTHER JONES (1830-1930)
Before a Congressional Committee on Labor Unrest

A frail, elderly woman, Mother Jones had a long career as an agitator for the rights of American working people. Without a fixed home, she moved from one working class community to another, leading protest marches against exploitation and unemployment. Frequently facing arrest and harassment, Mother Jones nevertheless played a prominent role as a United Mine Workers of America organizer who led strikes of coal miners in West Virginia, Pennsylvania, Colorado and Arizona. Her presence at the head of labor demonstrations frequently swayed public opinion in favor of the striking coal miners and gave the UMW a legitimacy which it might otherwise have lacked.

PHILIP MURRAY (1886-1952)

A Vice-president of the United Mine Workers Union, Philip Murray was appointed chairman of the Steel Workers Organizing Committee in 1936 by John L. Lewis, the President of the CIO. Under Murray's leadership, SWOC won collective bargaining agreements from such traditionally open-shop companies as U.S. Steel and Bethlehem Steel—agreements which transformed forever the relationship between the steel workers and the companies.

As the leader of SWOC, Murray became very well acquainted with the living conditions of unemployed steel workers and their families in hard-hit steel towns such as Braddock, Pennsylvania and Gary, Indiana. Here he gives a vivid description of the conditions which forced steel workers and their families to fight for a trade union.

OGDEN NASH (1902-1971)
"Pride Goeth Before a Raise"

Source: Seldes, *The Great Quotations*, p. 519.

Ogden Nash was an American poet and humorist who was for many years a writer for *The New Yorker* magazine. There he discovered his talent for writing witty verse and rhymes. "Pride Goeth Before a Raise" is a good example of his ability to poke fun at the social conscience of affluent Americans during the Great Depression.

JAMES OPPENHEIM (1882-1932)
"Bread and Roses"

Source: Milton Meltzer, *Bread and Roses, The Struggle of American Labor*, (New York: Alfred A. Knopf, 1967), p. 189.

On January 11, 1912, 23,000 Polish, Italian, French-Canadian, Russian-Jewish and Syrian immigrant textile workers in Lawrence, Massachusetts went on strike protesting a wage cut. Led by the IWW, the strikers' solidarity crossed ethnic lines and did not weaken in the face of police violence and harassment. After two months of bitter resistance, the woolen companies finally agreed to their demands.

The poet James Oppenheim was in Lawrence in 1912 and wrote the famous poem "Bread and Roses" after he saw a group of young mill girls picketing with a banner which read: "We want bread…And roses too!"

LUCY PARSONS (1853-1942)
Speech at the founding Convention of the IWW, June 1905

Source: Proceedings of the First Convention of the Industrial Workers of the World, June 27-July 8, 1905, (New York: Labor News Co., 1905).

A black woman, Lucy Parsons was the wife of Albert Parsons, one of four anarchists executed in 1887 for inciting the Haymarket Riot. Parsons wrote and lectured extensively in an effort, not only to clear her husband's name, but to spread the principles of socialism to American workers.

One of two women invited to speak at the founding convention of the IWW in 1905, Parsons urged the fledgling organization to concentrate its efforts on organizing women workers, particularly those employed in the textile industry.

PATERSON SILK STRIKE, 1913

Source: *Labor Scrap Book*, (ed.), Joe Glazer, Education Department United Rubber Workers of America, AFL-CIO, (Akron, n.d.), p. 7.

On February 25, 1913, 25,000 immigrant textile workers went on strike against Paterson, New Jersey's silk companies. During the lengthy and bitter strike, the workers held mass demonstrations against employers who compelled them to work ten hours a day for as little as six dollars a week.

Despite the heroic leadership of the IWW and the steadfast courage of the rank and file, mass arrests, lack of financial support, police harassment, and divisions between skilled and unskilled workers contributed to the strike's defeat. Nevertheless, the Paterson strike stands out as one of the most heroic struggles for justice in American labor history.

FRANCES PERKINS (1882-1965)

Source: Barbara Wertheimer, *We Were There, The Story of Working Women in America,* (New York: Pantheon Books, 1977), p. 313.

Appointed Secretary of Labor in 1933, Frances Perkins was the first woman member of a Presidential cabinet. This significant achievement, however, has obscured her early career as a champion of health and safety standards in American industry. After the tragic Triangle Fire of 1911, Perkins was appointed to aid the New York State Factory Investigating Committee in its inspection of New York's canneries and candy and paper box factories—industries which hired large numbers of women and children. Working conditions shocked many members of the Committee, and in their Second Report to the State Legislature, the Committee reported that "No words can express our condemnation of the inhuman greed and avarice that permits women to be this exploited." As a result of the Committee's work, the New York State Legislature passed the most comprehensive labor safety measures that had ever been placed on a state's statute books.

A. PHILIP RANDOLPH (1889-1979)

One of the most influential black trade unionists in the United States, A. Philip Randolph was in his youth a socialist, and was considered by Woodrow Wilson to be "the most dangerous Negro in America." Gradually dropping his socialist principles, Randolph nevertheless remained committed to the principles of social equality and trade unionism. In the 1920's Randolph organized and became President of the Brotherhood of Sleeping Car Porters, an all-black union. Randolph and the Brotherhood are best remembered for having organized the March On Washington Movement of 1941—the first time in American history that a black trade union assumed command of the national struggle for civil rights. The proposed march was designed to put pressure on the Federal Government to open new war-related industry jobs to blacks. The march, however, was called off after President Roosevelt signed a Federal Order prohibiting discrimination in Federal industries.

WALTER P. REUTHER (1907-1970)

Source: Frank Cormier and William J. Eaton, *Reuther,* (Englewood Cliffs: Prentice-Hall, 1970), p. vii.

Walter P. Reuther's impact is second only to John L. Lewis' in shaping the structure and character of the modern labor movement. A tool and die maker by trade, Reuther became an organizer for the United Auto Workers in Detroit in 1935 and became President of the union in 1946. For Reuther, trade unions were vehicles for social as well as economic reform, and under his leadership the UAW fought not only for higher wages and better working conditions, but for Civil Rights and justice for all working class Americans.

ELEANOR ROOSEVELT (1884-1962)

Source: Eleanor Roosevelt, "What are the Motives for a Woman Working When She Does Not Have To, For Income." Written for the January 1955 issue of *Charm,* but probably not published.

As America's First Lady, Eleanor Roosevelt symbolized the reforming spirit which pervaded America during the years of the New Deal. Her crusades for youth, blacks, women and the poor were well publicized in weekly press conferences, lectures, on radio programs and in newspaper columns.

Years before Betty Friedan revitalized the feminist movement, Eleanor Roosevelt was advocating the need for women to develop an identity of their own, outside of their traditional role as wives and mothers.

NICOLA SACCO (1891-1927)

Letter to Gardner Jackson, member of the Sacco and Vanzetti Defense Committee, June 14, 1927

Source: *The Letters of Sacco and Vanzetti*, Marion Frankfurter and Gardner Jackson, (eds.), (New York: Viking Press, 1928), p. 56.

Nicola Sacco and Bartolomeo Vanzetti (1888-1927) were two Italian anarchists who were arrested in 1920 on charges of murdering a shoe factory paymaster and guard at South Braintree, Massachusetts. Tried in an atmosphere of anti-radical hysteria, Sacco and Vanzetti were convicted on circumstantial evidence and were electrocuted on August 23, 1927. During the seven years of their incarceration, widespread doubt of their guilt inspired massive demonstrations on their behalf. Despite the fact that many books and articles have cast serious doubt on the evidence which convicted them, the State of Massachusetts has not officially exonerated them.

In a letter to Gardner Jackson, a correspondent for the *Boston Globe* and a member of the Defense Committee, Sacco declared that although men and women can be executed, their ideas can never be suppressed.

CARL SANDBURG (1878-1967)

Source: Carl Sandburg, *Chicago Poems*, (New York: Henry Holt and Co., 1916), p. 10.

A poet and biographer of Abraham Lincoln, Carl Sandburg left college without graduating and roamed America taking whatever odd jobs he could find. In his travels he became well acquainted with the values and life-styles of farm workers, cowboys and factory workers, and many of his poems are a tribute to their lives. In his book *Chicago Poems*, Sandburg voices somber concern over the debilitating effects of mill work on a young worker.

ROSE SCHNEIDERMAN (1884-1972)

Source: Wertheimer, *We Were There*, p. 312.

On March 26, 1911, a fire broke out on the upper floors of the Asch building in the non-union Triangle Waist factory off New York's Washington Square. Within minutes, 146 employees, mostly young Jewish and Italian girls, were burned to death inside locked doors.

Mass memorial protest meetings were held after the fire in which more than 50,000 people participated. Rose Schneiderman, then an organizer for the Women's Trade Union League, expressed the community's sense of moral outrage over working conditions that daily threatened the lives of young women.

MERLE TRAVIS (1917-   )

Source: Archie Green, *Only a Miner*, (Urbana: University of Illinois Press, 1972), p. 295.

Country singer/songwriter Merle Travis wrote "16 Tons" in the 1940s. Describing the desperate lives of coal miners in company-owned towns, "16 Tons" had a catchy melody and an irresistible rhythm which appealed to country and non-country music aficionados alike. Recorded by "Tennessee" Ernie Ford, the song became a big hit in the 1950s.

SOJOURNER TRUTH (1797-1883)

Source: Wertheimer, p. 140.

Born a slave, Sojourner Truth was a mystic who claimed
that she saw visions and heard voices imploring her to
become an itinerant preacher. Influenced by the religious
revivals of the 1830s, Sojourner Truth believed that people
were perfectable and could be divested of sin through
moral suasion. These beliefs led her into the abolitionist
movement and the struggle for women's suffrage.

The famous "Aren't I a Woman" speech was delivered
at a Women's Rights Convention in Akron, Ohio in 1854.
It was a vigorous reassertion of femininity from an ex-slave
whose hard life contradicted the Victorian image of proper
womanhood.

SAMUEL CLEMENS (Mark Twain, 1835-1910)

Source: Philip Foner, *Mark Twain, Social Critic*, New York: International
Publishers, 1958), p. 220.

Best known as a humorist and novelist, Mark Twain was
also an astute social critic. His letters and speeches
revealed an intellect that touched a wide variety of social,
economic and political issues. On the issue of trade
unionism, Twain made himself clear. Angered by the
growing monopolization of wealth and political power by
railroad companies and factory owners, Twain defended
the rights of workingmen to organize for the purpose of
claiming the full reward of their labor. In a speech to the
Monday Evening Club of Hartford, Connecticut in 1886,
Twain reaffirmed the rights of organizations such as the
Knights of Labor to exist as representatives of workingmen.

ART

BENNY ANDREWS
"Here Comes The Wind,"
    Hobert Grills
22½ x 28½
acrylic, collage and ink
    on paper

MARSHALL ARISMAN
A. Philip Randolph
35 x 40
oil on canvas

ROBERT ARNESON
Samuel Gompers
9½ x 17½ x 5½
glazed, fired ceramic

JACK BEAL
James Oppenheim
9³⁄₁₆ x 15⅝
pastel on gray paper

JUDY CHICAGO
Rose Schneiderman
16½ x 23½
colored pencil on paper

JACQUELINE CHWAST
Eleanor Roosevelt
9¼ x 12¾
cut paper

SEYMOUR CHWAST
Ogden Nash
11 x 15½
mixed media on chipboard

SUE COE
Akron Sit-down Striker
18⁵⁄₁₆ x 25½
gouache on paper

JOHN COLLIER
Carl Sandburg, "Mill Doors"
16¹⁵⁄₁₆ x 23¼
pastel on paper

PAUL DAVIS
Job
10 x 13¾
acrylic on illustration board

RALPH FASANELLA
"City Street," Philip Murray
39⅞ x 30
oil on canvas

AUDREY FLACK
Sojourner Truth
48 x 62
acrylic on canvas

MILTON GLASER
Nicola Sacco
17⅞ x 23⅞
ink on paper

MIMI GROSS
"Greetings from Silver Lake,"
    Walter P. Reuther
27¾ x 22⅜ x 9 (approx.)
mixed media construction

ROBERT GROSSMAN
Merle Travis
11¼ x 15
gouache on illustration board

PHILIP HAYS
Woody Guthrie
16⅞ x 21⅞
watercolor on
    illustration board

BRAD HOLLAND
Martin Luther King, Jr.
9⅜ x 12⅜
oil on board

LUIS JIMENEZ, JR.
Thomas Jefferson
35⅞ x 27¾
colored pencil on paper

WILLIAM KING
Abraham Lincoln
19½ x 72 x 15
vinyl on aluminum frame

JACOB LAWRENCE
"Builders," Mark Twain
18½ x 25½
gouache on paper

DANIEL MAFFIA
Knights of Labor motto
18 x 22⁹⁄₁₆
watercolor and wax
    on newsprint

ED McGOWIN
"Mother Mary Jones"
46 x 62 x 31
mixed media sculpture

JAMES McMULLAN
Joe Hill
9¼ x 12¾
watercolor on paper

ALICE NEEL
Frances Perkins
18 x 24
oil on canvas

BARBARA NESSIM
Paterson Silk Strike banner
10½ x 14⅞
watercolor on paper

HONORÉ SHARRER
George Meany
19⅜ x 25⅜
casein on paper

ANITA SIEGEL
Eugene V. Debs
13¾ x 19⅛
collage on paper

EDWARD SOREL
"Children Breaking Coal,"
    George Baer
11⅝ x 15⅞
ink and watercolor on paper

MAY STEVENS
"We are the Slaves of Slaves,"
    Lucy Parsons
21¾ x 27¾
mixed media on board

ANTON van DALEN
"Open Shop," John L. Lewis
36 x 48
oil on linen

ROBERT WEAVER
Frederick Douglass
17⅞ x 25¼
acrylic and pencil
    on illustration board

MIRIAM WOSK
"Mixed Greens," Roberto Acuna
35 x 51 x 4¾
mixed media construction

CREDITS

Photographs by Bobby Hanson,
New York, except as noted.
Page 55 (Ralph Fasanella) by
Quesada/Burke and page 19
(Audrey Flack) by D. James Dee.

Type for this book was set in
Cheltenham Old Style by Haber
Typographers, Inc., New York.

Lithography by Sterling Roman
Press, Inc., New York.

Separations by Prolith International,
Inc., Beltsville, Maryland.

Paper stock is Warren Cameo Dull,
60# cover, supplied by Marquardt
and Company, Incorporated,
New York.

Union-made paper by members of
United Paperworkers International
Union/AFL-CIO/CLC.